Cookin' for Your Canine:
Healthy Recipes for Happy Dogs

Cheryl Bauer

To Bill, marge, Chloe & Roxi,
BON APÉTIT!!

10 Dogs Later...

Cheryl Bauer

10 Dogs Later Publishing

Book design: Erika M. Schreck and Cheryl Bauer
Editing: Erika M. Schreck, www.erikaschreck.com; Ken Chez
Proofreading: Erika M. Schreck, Ken Chez and MaryAnn Briggs
Cover design: Erika M. Schreck

Cheryl Bauer is not a medical doctor or veterinarian. This book is not intended as a substitute for the medical advice or treatment from a veterinarian. The reader should regularly consult a veterinarian for his/her dog with matters relating to health and nutrition, particularly with respect to any symptoms that may require diagnosis or medical attention. The intent of the author is only to offer information of a general nature to help the reader in his/her quest for dog health and well-being. In the event the reader uses any of the information in this book, which is his/her constitutional and individual right, the author and the publisher assume no responsibility for the reader's actions or results.

Printed in the USA
First Edition, September 2016

Library of Congress Cataloging-in-Publication Data
Bauer, Cheryl
    Cookin' for your canine: healthy recipes for happy dogs / Cheryl Bauer
        p. cm.
1. Dogs. 2. Cooking. 3. Health.

ISBN-13: 978-0-692-73729-3

"The greatness of a nation and its moral progress
can be judged by the way its animals are treated."
Ghandi

This book is dedicated to the wonder dogs, Shelby and Skye.

And to all of the beautiful dogs who have shared our lives,
live in our hearts and have irrevocably made us
more compassionate, caring and loving human beings
to the world at large.

Acknowledgements

A big, resounding THANKS to...

First, foremost and forever, the multi-talented, brilliant Erika Schreck. Without her friendship, direction, editing and just plain old help with EVERYTHING, I would never have been able to turn my ideas into this book. Thank you a million times, and it's still not enough!

My husband Ken Chez for embracing my crazy dog lady side and supporting me on this adventure. Thank you for being my partner in life, love, the kitchen and dog parenting, and supporting my vision for this book.

Mary Huffman for donating her generous time and energy to creating *and* initiating a video interview and instructional cooking demo--and we had so much fun! My heart lights up when I think about how much she cared with helping get my message out with producing these videos. Her efforts continued by offering my products with her holiday gifts. Thanks, Op!

My friends and family for thinking this was a great idea and supporting me with your cheerleading and creative thoughts. Especially Diana and Rick Witherspoon, Stacy Boston, Theresa Kulstad and MaryAnn Briggs.

Marilyn Woods-Brown, Mary Jo Berte and Felicia Dumont for their contributions and expertise about nutrition and alternative healing modalities for dogs.

Auguste Escoffier School of Culinary Arts, Boulder, for teaching me invaluable cooking skills, which further ignited my love to cook and strengthened my confidence with creating my own recipes.

And...to all the dogs I have loved in my lifetime, whether mine or not, you have made my heart, and my life, bigger, better and brighter.

Table of Contents

Table of Contents

Helpful Hint

Helpful Hints

Introduction

Look at who you were when you were young and what you were drawn to, and you'll probably notice like I did that those passions often follow you through life. My love of dogs started very early. I was born in Maryland and lived there with my parents and older brother, Kenny—now known as Frank. My parents, Boo and Betty, had a beagle named Booty—you can't make this stuff up!—who lived with them before my brother and I came along. He absolutely hated us. He would nip and growl at us, when he wasn't downright ignoring us, and we LOVED him. You would think we would have ended up being afraid of dogs, but dog love was in our DNA.

One year, on Christmas Eve, my father came home and surprised us by pulling a kitten out of the bomber jacket he was wearing. Knowing how much my brother and I loved animals, our parents enjoyed surprising us with kittens, gerbils and hamsters, and while we loved them wholeheartedly, my brother and I were always dog crazy.

On the weekends, my brother and I, when our ages were still in the single digits, would get up hours before our parents and go out and find neighborhood dogs and cats and bring them into the house. Mom and Dad were very tolerant and amused, but once when we brought a cat into the house that turned out to be vicious, they had a hard time removing it from our house, and *that was the end of that*. Our whole family loved animals, but my father had a disability and could not walk long distances, so we had many cats after Booty but never any dogs.

When I was about six years old, I was given an Easy-Bake Oven for Christmas. That oven was my prized possession, and I would happily whip up miniature cakes cooked by a light bulb all day long.

Now look at me: I'm finally putting the two together and writing a cookbook for dogs!

"Acquiring a dog may be the only time
a person gets to chose a relative."
Mordecai Siegel

"Everyone thinks they have the best dog....
and none of them are wrong."
W.R. Purche

Meet the Tasters

"Until one has loved an animal,
a part of one's soul remains unawakened."
Anatole France

Shelby

Breed: Black Lab
Age: 9½ years
Nicknames: Princess, Shelly Belly, Shel-Belle

Shelby came to us from the Humane Society when she was two years old. She is a long-standing member of Tennis Balls Anonymous. A great actress! When she doesn't want to do something, she plays damsel in distress. Nicknamed "Shiny Shelby" by the vet tech because of her beautiful, shiny, black coat. Great snuggler. Always up for an adventure. Excellent at manifesting belly rubs. Great massage room apprentice, usually snoring through the session and then shaking her body and head when she hears the singing bowls at the end—time to go! Picky about her friends, but 100% devoted. Her favorite things.... belly rubs, tennis balls, chasing bunnies, Kongs with liverwurst, morning snuggling before getting out of bed… but most of all… her beloved SkyeBoy.

Skye

Breed: Golden Retriever
Age: 12½ years
Nicknames: SkyeBoy

Big, beautiful paws and an adorable puppy face, even at 12½! An old soul, he is a friend to every person and dog he meets. A people magnet. Loves to play, walk, hike, swim and travel to new places, as long as he doesn't have to get in the car—he *hates* car rides! And, he ONLY sits in the front seat, no matter if someone else is already sitting there... non-negotiable. He does everything using the least energy possible, including swimming and chasing bunnies, squirrels and deer. He is food-obsessed and tries to hypnotize you to give him a bite of whatever you may be eating. His favorite walk is to the tennis courts with his beloved Shelby and stealing her tennis balls.

Luna
Breed: Chocolate Lab/Australian Shepherd
Age: 5 years
Nickname(s): Baby Girl

Luna is a darling with a penchant for all things FOOD! A certified Therapy Dog, Luna has weekly stints at the hospital and makes appearances as a R.E.A.D. (Reading Education Assistance Dog) in local elementary schools. This baby girl loves to swim and will find a way to make a trickle of water seem like a lake. Her "eyebrows" are like double windows into her sweet soul, and her ability to splay her back legs into a froggy position make her everybody's darling. She's a talker, too!

Ella
Breed: Black Lab
Age: 11 years
Nickname(s): El

Ella was rescued as a Hurricane Katrina dog. She is from a long line of owners until she had the good fortune to end up with Mary Lee, owner of PC's Pantry for Dogs and Cats in Boulder, Colorado. She is the sweetest thing, with the sweetest face. Due to her traumatic experience, she is terrified of storms and high-tails it inside if there is even a hint of bad weather. She loves her siblings Forrest and Mini.

Mini
Breed: Chihuahua
Age: 14 years
Nickname(s): Worm

Mini was found running down Colfax Street in Denver as a stray. Her teeth were bad, and she had lost an eye. She is shy but oh so sweet and loves to be held and cuddled. Her owner Mary Lee says that Mini hates having her picture taken. She's not kidding! Every time someone aims a camera at Mini, she averts her face and twisted her body away. We still think she is a beautiful girl, inside and out.

Tilly
Breed: Standard Poodle
Age: 8 years
Nickname(s): Till Till

Chantilly Margeaux Lacy—"Tilly"—is from a litter of pup rescues, and she picked her owner! Tilly is the sweetest and is as silly as they get! She loves everyone and has a glowing disposition. Romping and playing like a floppy rag doll, she brings so much joy and happiness with every wet kiss and warm snuggle. With the perfect pup comes imperfection: Tilly is a famous turkey burger thief, as she once counter-surfed and inhaled three right out of the pan!

Forrest
Breed: Saint Bernard
Age: 8 years
Nickname(s): Boops

Forrest was given his name because when he was adopted, Mary Lee was told he was found in a forest. We later learned the story wasn't true, but the name stuck! He had luxating patellas when he was a puppy and couldn't walk. Now he is big and strong and loves to go on long walks. He likes to talk and tilts his head sideways when listening; when told to use his inside voice, he lowers the volume. He prefers his humans clean and nice-smelling, not stinky and dirty—seriously!

JamieLee

Breed: Labrador Retriever Mix
Age: 14½ years
Nicknames: Jamie

When Jamie's DogMom was reading the *New York Times* about 14½ years ago, she saw an ad with Jamie Lee Curtis as a spokesperson for AT&T and remembered that DogDaddy has a huge crush on this actress. The name JamieLee stuck. As a youngster, Jamie's favorite activities were stealing other dogs' toys, especially their frisbees, and playing soccer. Squirrel-chasing was also one of her happiest times. Jamie enjoys daily walks and sometimes sleeps 18 hours a day. She also now sports white eyebrows, muzzle, paws and butt.

Harley

Breed: Golden Retriever
Age: 11
Nicknames: Sweet Boy, Zen Harley,
Harley Barley

Harley was rescued from a golden retriever rescue in Colorado and has often made people question, "Is Harley even a dog? He's so calm, and he has such a healing, intuitive presence!" A gentle, loving, sensitive soul, Harley seems to impress everyone he meets. He's a favorite with children and a stress-reliever for all, especially when he joins his guardian at her office for reiki sessions she offers. He is a unique, amazing companion for his mama and loves to travel, camp, babysit and run.

Massage for Your Dog

As a massage therapist, I highly recommend massage to help maintain and improve the health of your dog. You can tell when you've found a good spot to massage when your pooch actually presses into your fingers. If they pull away, you may be applying too much pressure. Less is more! With animals, use a light, slow touch that is significantly less than the pressure you would use on a human. Pay attention to the signals your dog is sending.

There are acupressure points that you can stimulate with your fingers, which will benefit your dog:

UB 40 (Bend Middle) is located on the hind leg in the middle of the depression behind the knee. It is an excellent place to lightly rub to help relieve pain and stiffness in the back, knee and hip.

GB 20 (Wind Pool) is located in a depression on either side of the nape of the neck, at the base of the skull, behind the back of the ears. This point is good for eye irritation, seizures, colds and allergies.

LI 11 (Pool at the Bend) is found when you flex your dog's front leg and locate the point at the end of the elbow crease. This point helps regulate the immune system, and is an anti-inflammatory point in the upper body, helping lower fever, pain and swelling.

Ingredients and Supplements Nutritional Information

"If your dog is overweight, it means
you aren't getting enough exercise."
Unknown

Foods That Are Toxic to Dogs

Never Feed Your Dog the Following

Avocado
Chocolate
Garlic
Grapes
Macadamia nuts
Moldy foods
Onions
Raisins
Raw bread dough
Tomatoes
Xylitol – found in sugar-free gum

Note from Cheryl
Over the years, I've learned from experts to keep certain foods out of my dogs' diet. While you may have these foods in your household, they should not be fed to your dog. You will not find any of these ingredients in the recipes included in this book.

Foods and Supplements:
Nutritional Value for Dogs

> ### Please Note
> Always check with your vet to verify what is best for your dog, especially if health concerns exist.

Apples

Apples with the skins on are full of plant chemicals—phytonutrients—that are thought to be protective against some types of cancers in humans. They are a great source of vitamins A and C, and fiber.

Avoid letting your dog eat the entire apple, especially the core, as apple seeds contain cyanide. Though the effects of a few apple seeds will likely not harm your dog, it's better to avoid feeding dogs the apple core.

Berries

Blackberries, strawberries and blueberries are the holy trinity of healthy berries for your trusty mutt. These berries are loaded with antioxidants to fight free radicals in your dog, and they also have plenty of fiber and vitamins. Berries contain quercetin, a plant pigment which decreases joint inflammation, and they aid weight loss, protect the heart and help ward off cancer. Additionally, strawberries contain an enzyme that can help whiten your dog's teeth.

Keep a bag of frozen strawberries, blueberries or blackberries in your freezer to have a crunchy snack on hand for your dog. Just don't feed unlimited amounts because even though the sugar in strawberries is natural sugar, too much can be harmful.

Chia Seeds

Chia has three times the number of Omega-3 fatty acids as salmon! Having Omega-3 is important to balance out Omega-6 fatty acids and promotes healthy cells, immune system, skin and coat, and joints. Chia seeds also develop and maintain a dog's brain and eyes.

Chia seeds can reduce inflammation, too! Additionally, soaking chia seeds in water can prevent blood sugar spikes—see instructions below.

Author Suggestion: Gelatinous Chia Seeds Instructions

Add about ¼ cup chia seeds to one cup of water; stir and let this mixture sit for at least an hour, and the seeds will develop a gelatinous coating. You may keep this mixture in your refrigerator for about a week, adding small amounts to your dog's kibble or using amounts specified in recipes in this book.

Chia Seeds are Fiber-Rich

If your dog's bowel movements are a concern, increasing dietary fiber through adding gelatinous chia seeds can help. Fiber can alleviate constipation, and also help with regularity and weight loss. Dogs who suffer from obstructed anal sacs will also benefit from more fiber.

Eggs

Eggs are a very digestible protein and a great source of riboflavin, which is vitamin B2, which promotes energy and red blood cell growth, and helps slow the aging process. Many experts recommend cooking the egg, such as scrambling or poaching. Usually up to a few eggs per week for a large dog is a safe bet.

For dogs who are prone to digestive upset, eggs can provide a little protein boost. *As a frequent and healthy go-to mix-in for my dogs' kibble,* I add some boneless, skinless sardines and a *cooked* egg, and they love it!

Flaxseed

When flaxseed is ground, it releases oil, which contains fiber and protein. These tiny, brown or gold seeds have a pleasant, nutty flavor. When consumed, it can aid in preventing digestive illnesses and provide powerful anti-inflammatory, antioxidant, antifungal and anti-cancer benefits. Using flaxseed has also been known to help improve your dog's skin and coat. Flax may be eaten safely by all members of the family, including dogs.

Feeding Flaxseed

You may want to ask your veterinarian about the proper amount of flaxseed to feed your dog. Flaxseed can be purchased in its natural form or in liquid, capsule or ground form; however, **do not feed your dog whole flaxseed**. While whole flaxseed won't hurt your dog, it's most likely to pass right through, undigested. Grinding the seeds with a spice or coffee grinder releases important nutrients. Refrigerating the flaxseed will keep them fresh and prevent them from becoming rancid. Grind the seeds daily or weekly and then refrigerate. You may sprinkle a teaspoon or two of ground flaxseed over your dog's food, depending on your dog's weight.

If you love to make your own homemade dog biscuits, you can bake the ground flaxseed into the biscuits because flaxseed has been found to be stable even after a few hours of baking.

Garbanzo Beans

Garbanzo beans are a great source of magnesium (supports cell function), Vitamin A (sustains eye health), potassium (supports heart, muscles, nerves and kidneys) and protein. They are very beneficial for digestion, eye health and heart health.

I prefer to use quick-and-easy canned garbanzo beans, and I always make sure to rinse and drain them. Typically, garbanzo beans are mashed with a fork or ground in a food processor.

Kale

Kale is a great source of Vitamin A, D and K, as well as minerals like copper, potassium and iron. Kale's antioxidant and anti-inflammatory benefits are primarily linked to the high concentration of these vitamins and phytonutrients, which help promote liver health. Rich in lutein, kale also supports eye health. Additionally, some research has shown that kale can be effective in helping prevent some forms of cancer, including colon and bladder cancer.

If you are feeding kale to your dog often, make sure your dog is getting enough calcium because kale contains oxalates that interfere with the absorption of calcium. Include foods that supply calcium to dogs and are a good addition to meals, including yogurt, spinach, beans, sweet potatoes, broccoli, salmon, tuna, sardines or trout.

Oats

Oatmeal has been proven to have a very low glycemic index; high-quality and organic oats are uncontaminated by other grains and considered gluten free. Oats are important in controlling blood sugar levels and reducing digestive issues for pets. Some vets feel that the protein in oatmeal is less likely to cause an allergic reaction and therefore can be an ideal nutrient included in a diet formulated for pets suspected of having food sensitivity or allergies. Due to its fiber content, pound for pound, oatmeal contains fewer carbohydrate calories than other grains, making it an ideal ingredient to support weight management as well as healthy bowel function.

Pumpkin

Pumpkin is a good source of fiber, which maintains intestinal and gut health. Pumpkin also contains beta-carotene, a source of Vitamin A, which supports the eyes and vision, healthy skin and the immune system. Interestingly, a small bit of pumpkin added to a dog's kibble can assist a dog who is either constipated or has diarrhea. *If your dog has diarrhea,* cooked white rice and a bit of pumpkin create a go-to meal.

Sardines

Sardines are a great addition to your dog's diet! Rich in omega-3 fatty acids, sardines help maintain your dog's immune system, hormones, heart and eyes. Sardines also help with arthritis, lower cholesterol, fight cancer, and repair and support soft tissue. Full of vitamins, minerals and nutrients, sardines have been considered one of the safest fish you can give your dog and one of the world's healthiest foods. Furthermore, sardines support a healthy coat, blood function, circulation and appetite for dogs.

Be sure to give your dog sustainably caught, boneless sardines, packed in either water or olive oil. Generally, small dogs can be given up to one can per week, divided among several meals and along with their kibble, while large dogs can have up to two cans per week, divided among meals and along with their kibble. If you have more than one dog, they can share!

Spices

If you would like to spice up your dog's life, spices can add flavor to foods and offer a lot of nutritional value for our dogs. Spices can be an important part of your pet's diet and can boost their immune system and/or fight disease.

Note for all spices: Make sure you know the importance of possible side-effects and the correct, safe dosage of any herb or spice you may give to your dog, as you do not want to harm your pet. Remember: a little goes a long way when feeding spices to your dog. I recommend starting with ⅛-¼ teaspoon of any of these spices, depending on the size of your dog.

- *Caraway Seeds*

Caraway seeds are rich in dietary fiber, vital vitamins, minerals and antioxidants (fight cancer and disease). Caraway seeds are also good for muscle health (anti-contraction). They bulk out food and help prevent constipation. Caraway seeds can be used whole or ground when adding to your dog's food.

- *Cinnamon*

Cinnamon is a powerful antioxidant! One teaspoon of cinnamon contains as many antioxidants as half a cup of blueberries, and it also has antibacterial and antifungal properties. It has been helpful for dealing with gastrointestinal problems, such as nausea, diarrhea and flatulence.

- *Fennel Seeds*

Fennel seeds have mainly been used to calm the digestive tract, treat flatulence, clean the liver, detoxify the body and act as a natural diuretic. They can help normalize the appetite and aid weight loss in dogs.

Spices continued

Fennel seeds have also been known to ease arthritis due to their antioxidant and anti-inflammatory properties. You may serve fennel seeds to your dog by sprinkling a few whole seeds in your dog's kibble.

- *Ginger*
Ginger is a great digestive aid, as it can help increase the production of digestive fluids and saliva, therefore helping relieve indigestion, gas, nausea, stomach cramps and diarrhea. If your dog has motion sickness, ginger dog treats can help settle his or her stomach. Ginger is also known as an anti-inflammatory and can help relieve arthritis pain.

- *Turmeric*
This spice is anti-inflammatory and antimicrobial, and is widely recognized for its anti-cancerous properties. Turmeric calms itchy skin, lessens allergies and helps control arthritis. Most dogs like the taste of turmeric, and a pinch can easily be sprinkled on your dog's food.

Spaghetti Squash

Spaghetti squash is a nutritional, high-fiber, low-calorie vegetable. It is loaded with beta carotene, which is great for your dog's eyes, and the fiber keeps your dog feeling full without a lot of additional calories. Spaghetti squash is also great to add to your dog's kibble for weight management. Other squashes are perfectly fine to use, but they have a higher starch content.

Sweet Potatoes

Sweet potatoes contain the highest amino acid content of any of its cousins in the starch family. Amino acids are essential in your dog's diet to maintain healthy, strong, lean muscles. The amino acids also increase the body's antioxidant activity. Antioxidants are essential for ridding the body of free radicals that can cause cancer and other harmful diseases.

Research has shown that sweet potatoes also help rid the liver of fatty cells and keep vital organs healthy. Their high fiber content is great for the digestive system.

When adding to your dog's kibble, cut one to two sweet potatoes into bite-size pieces and bake for 30-45 minutes or until soft at 350°F. Add a few baked and cooled pieces to a small dog's kibble and up to a palm-size of pieces to a large dog's kibble.

When offering as a snack, slice a sweet potato thinly and spread slices on baking sheet on an ungreased *or* very lightly greased baking sheet and bake for two hours or until chewy and firm consistency at 250 degrees. These snack slices will shrink to about half their size as they bake.

Vitamins

- *Beta-Carotene*
  Beta-carotene works as an antioxidant, helping to prevent disease and infection. Its role as a precursor of vitamin A makes it important for healthy skin and hair coat, normal bone development, general eye health and cancer prevention. Foods to consider adding to your dog's diet that contain beta-carotene include carrots, yams, spinach, kale, sweet potatoes, winter squash, cantaloupe and apricots. **Real foods versus synthetic vitamins are most often considered a better choice.**

- *Omega-3s*
  Omega-3's are beneficial in so many ways, including the following:
  - control allergies and skin disease
  - maintain mental alertness in older dogs
  - maintain healthy and shiny coat
  - benefit the skin
  - encourage proper eye health
  - alleviate symptoms of inflammatory diseases
  - assist certain cardiovascular problems in dogs, such as high blood pressure and abnormal, rapid heart rhythms
  - slow development and spread of certain cancer tumors
  - improve the immune system

Vitamins continued

There are fish oil supplements made specifically for dogs, or you can use the same supplements you use for yourself, but make sure they do not contain added omega-6s. *Always check with your vet for dosage recommendations.* Dogs need a supplement high in omega-3s, but the added omega-6 can upset the balance of the fats in your pet's system.

Unless your dog is allergic to fish, omega-3 from fish oils such as salmon oil, cod liver oil and sardine oil is always better than omega-3 from plant sources. Special enzymes, which dogs do not have, are required to convert the inactive omega-3s from plant sources into the active omega-3 forms, while fatty acids contained in fish oil are readily assimilated.

Pets with allergies may require higher dosages than the standard dosage; check with your vet for safe and proper dosage. You can either add the liquid form or puncture a capsule of omega-3 to add to your dog's food. If you exceed his or her capacity to absorb it, your dog may get diarrhea. Generally, in three to six weeks, you will likely see an improvement in your pet's coat, which indicates a healthier pet.

- *Vitamin C*

Vitamin C can be a possible supplement for your dog for greater resistance to disease and a better ability to recover from injuries or illness.

Sometimes Vitamin C is prescribed by holistic veterinarians for a number of illnesses, such as cancer, kennel cough and other respiratory infections, exposure to contagious diseases, abscesses and other bacterial infections. Due to its important role with increasing collagen production, Vitamin C appears to be especially helpful for slowing—and possibly reversing—degenerative joint disease, hip dysplasia and spinal disorders.

Professionals sometimes suggest giving dogs Vitamin C before and after vaccinations, and for healthy teeth and gums. It also helps increase serotonin, which helps fight depression. And, yes, dogs can get depressed!

Yogurt

Yogurt can be an allergen for some dogs, so don't overdo it—a teaspoon or tablespoon will suffice, depending on the weight of your dog.

It's a good source of calcium and protein. Only use yogurt that has live active bacteria, no sugars and no artificial sweeteners.

The active bacteria in yogurt may act as a probiotic, which is very helpful if your dog has digestive issues. If you need to be mindful about your dog's weight, choose a fat-free yogurt *without* fat substitutes like Simplesse® or Olestra.

A nice summer treat is to put some yogurt in a ramekin or similar half-cup, small dish and freeze it. You can add some gelatinous chia seeds (see p. 16), flaxseed and/or blue to make this healthy treat more beneficial. This treat will take a while for your dog to eat, like a doggie ice cream cone!

Helpful Hint

Protecting Your Dog's Paws

Your dogs pick up many allergens and irritants through their paws. In the United States, where many lawns and trees are treated with pesticides in the spring and summer, dogs can pick up these poisons on a daily walk. In the winter months, where salt and other chemicals are used to treat the roads and sidewalks for ice, dogs can get salt granules embedded in their paws. What can you do?

I like to add about a half cup of Epsom salts to a gallon of warm water in a large bowl or bucket, similar to a dishwashing tub with a flat bottom. Then, after mixing the water and salts until the salts are dissolved, carefully place one or more of your dog's paws in the water, fully submerged for several minutes. Avoid letting your dog drink any of this water! Have a towel nearby to immediately dry the soaking paw(s). If your dog will not tolerate this approach, you may also soak a towel with the Epsom salt water, wiping and wrapping your dog's paws. Dog booties are another option for the winter time!

"Dogs are the leaders of the planet.
If you see two life forms, one of them's making
a poop, the other one's carrying it for him,
who would you assume is in charge?"
Jerry Seinfield

Stomach Distress

Harley is an 11-year-old golden retriever, and he has had a sensitive stomach since he was a puppy. Sometimes he vomits or gets intestinal distress, either for unknown reasons or because he ingested something outside that upset his system.

Whenever your dog has similar or related challenges, here are some good things to have on hand that are bland and easy on the stomach:

> bananas
> blueberries
> boiled white rice*
> broccoli—baked, steamed or cooked
> sweet potatoes—baked and mashed
> noodles/pasta—cooked
> oats
> canned 100% pure pumpkin*
> lean meat—cooked and drained, such as turkey, skinless chicken or beef
> meat-based baby food with no onions or garlic
> sweet potato—baked
> plain yogurt, without sugars

> *quick-boil white rice and canned pumpkin are recommended staples for any dog owner's pantry

If Your Dog Is Vomiting Or Has Diarrhea

If your dog is vomiting or has diarrhea, the go-to meal is boiled rice, 100% pure pumpkin and low-fat meat, such as white-meat chicken, turkey, buffalo or extra-lean ground beef. Mix three (3) parts rice to one (1) part meat, along with up to two tablespoons of pumpkin, and serve over three to four small meals during the day.

One of the things you need to look for is dehydration, since vomiting and diarrhea dehydrate the body. You can check your dog's gums by doing the following: press on the gums until the area becomes white; then, count how long it takes for the gums' surface to return to normal, which takes about 1.5 seconds for color to return. If it takes longer, your dog may be dehydrated. I have poured unflavored Pedialyte into my dog's water bowls when she was dehydrated because this product contains potassium and electrolytes.

If your dog likes ice cubes, you could make ice cubes made with water, coconut water or unflavored Pedialyte, and some bite-size pieces of cantaloupe, watermelon and/or blueberries, which are high-water fruits good for their digestion.

Suggested Recipes and Ingredients for Stomach Distress

If your dog is experiencing stomach distress—upset stomach or diarrhea, consider consulting the Harley's Happy Tummy Bake (p. 48) and Healthy Belly Cookies (pp. 39-40) recipes. These recipes are intended for dogs who may have stomach sensitivity and could inspire supplemental ingredients for your dog's kibble.

Allergies, Inflammation and Irritants

Pets can get itchy during spring, summer or fall, which can be a sign of seasonal environmental allergies. If symptoms continue year round, they are most likely allergic to something in their diet or something in their home or environment.

Omega-3 fatty acids help decrease inflammation in the body while your dog is fighting allergies. The best sources of omega-3s are chia seeds (see pp. 15-16), salmon oil, tuna oil and other fish oils. See pp. 21-22 for more information about omega-3 source and dosage guidelines. Because foods high in carbohydrates can trigger inflammation, eliminating or reducing grains from your dog's diet can help reduce inflammation.

Recipes

"If you think dogs can't count, try putting three dog biscuits
in your pocket and then give him only two of them."
Phil Pastoret

Things You Need to Know...

1. All cooking temperatures for these recipes are in Fahrenheit.

2. Remember that there are certain foods you should never feed your dog. Please refer to this list on p. 14.

3. My favorite brands for baking ingredients are King Arthur Flour and Bob's Red Mill®. Both of these brands can be found at your local grocery store.

4. If available, feed your dog high-quality, preferably organic, humanely raised meats, seafood, fruits and vegetables. I do not feed my dogs food that I would not eat.

5. If your dog is on a grain-free diet, use the alternate, gluten-free flour provided in recipes that use flour.

6. If a recipe calls for using an appliance you don't have, you can still achieve the same effects with alternatives. For example, a blender will suffice for a food processor. If you don't have a steamer, you may use stainless steel colander in a sizeable stove pot with a cover. A fork can replace a whisk, and so forth.

7. For any recipe involving baking, make sure that oven is already preheated before you start baking. If you don't, baking time and quality will be affected.

8. Most recipes do not take more than 10-15 minutes to put together, not including cooking time.

9. To ensure quality and longevity of the delicious meals and treats you're making for your dog, make sure you refrigerate anything you make, in a sealed container.

10. As I did, when you start cooking and baking more for your canine, you will get more comfortable with creating your own dishes and determining your own substitutes and preferences.

Recipes

Snacks

"A dog wags its tail with its heart."
Martin Buxbaum

Cool Off with Ice Pops

*If your dog likes ice cubes, this is a treat and
a great way to get some extra nutrition into their day!*

✳ Ingredients
1 cup cubed pineapple
1 banana
1 cup coconut water

✳ Supplies
ice cube tray—I like the trays with the XL cubes
food processor or blender

Instructions
1. Add all ingredients to a food processor or blender; blend until mixture is smooth.

2. Pour mixture into ice cube tray and freeze.

Variations
Watermelon and blueberries are also great fruits to substitute if your dog has had digestive issues, as both of these fruits are very hydrating. Use one cup of each fruit and one cup of liquid, such as water, coconut water or unflavored Pedialyte. Blend and freeze.

Tasty Training Treats

Throw a handful of these in your pocket to help train your dog on walks.

✳ Ingredients

2 cups cooked, chopped chicken, hamburger, bison or seafood
¼ cup whole wheat flour (if using gluten-free flour, add one extra TBSP)
2 TBSP ground flaxseed
½ carrot grated
½ cup chicken broth

✳ Supplies

two standard-size baking sheets
parchment paper or silpats

✳ Instructions

1. Preheat oven to 350 degrees.

2. Line two baking sheets with parchment paper or silpats.

3. Add all ingredients to food processor and mix well. Refrigerate mixture 10-15 minutes; chilling the mixture will make forming the treats much easier because the mixture will be firmer and easier to work with.

4. Using a ¼ tsp. for smaller dogs OR a ½ tsp. for medium to large dogs, place mounds of mixture on baking sheet within one inch of each other.

5. Bake for 30 minutes, switching pans halfway through.

6. Cool. Place in re-sealable container or bag and keep refrigerated.

This recipe yields nearly two full baking sheets.

Kitchen Sink Cookies

You know that expression "everything but the kitchen sink"?
These cookies are made with whatever you already have in the kitchen. Here we go!

✳ Ingredients

1 lb of ground meat—anything but pork
2 cups of veggies, cut into very small pieces, i.e. broccoli, sweet
potato, squash, carrots
2 TBSP *ground* seeds, i.e. flaxseed, pumpkin seeds, chia seeds
½ cup of fruit, cut into small pieces, i.e. berries, banana, apple
2 eggs
1¼ cups cold water
½ tsp. of baking soda
4 cups whole wheat flour (if using gluten-free flour, add 4½ cups)—
with an additional ¼ cup of either flour for dusting

✳ Supplies

two to three baking sheets
large mixing bowl and utensil for mixing (ex. wooden spoon)
parchment paper or silpat
rolling pin
cookie cutters—or small, round drinking glass

✳ Instructions

1. Preheat oven to 350 degrees.

2. *If you don't have the time or energy to steam or bake the veggies to
   soften:* Grate raw vegetables, such as carrots and squash, and/or dice
   other raw vegetables, such as spinach or kale. *If you're baking or steaming
   the veggies to soften:* Bake veggies on a baking sheet for approximately 30
   minutes at 350 degrees. If using steamer, steam veggies for 20-30
   minutes. Let cool. Cut into small pieces.

3. If you're baking or steaming the veggies, make this your first step. While
   the veggies are cooking, start browning the meat. As the meat is
   browning, combine the flour, seeds, fruit and eggs in a large mixing

Kitchen Sink Cookies continued

bowl until thoroughly combined. If you're not baking or steaming your veggies, grate and cut while the meat is browning.

4. Add cooked, drained and cooled meat, veggies and 1¼ cup cold water to the ingredients in the large mixing bowl. Combine well. This mixture should form a big ball.

If it is too wet and not forming a ball, add more flour. If too dry and crumbly, add a bit more water. Once you have a well-mixed and ball-shaped combination, put the large bowl in the fridge for 10-15 minutes or more, which makes it easier to handle and to roll out.

5. Line two baking pans with parchment paper or silpats. Sprinkle flour on clean counter or large cutting board. Divide mixture in half. Take half and place on sprinkled flour, and add a bit more flour to this dough. With a rolling pin, roll dough until it's about ¼" or slightly less thick.

Periodically sprinkle flour on top of rolled mixture as you're rolling it out and whenever dough is sticking to the rolling pin; then, flip the dough over. For the other half of dough, you will either repeat these steps while the first batch is baking, or freeze the dough for later for up to a month for your dog's deliciousness.

6. Cookie-cutting time! It's more fun if you have cute cookie cutters, but if you don't, you can use the open end a small, round drinking glass. Once you have two trays full of cut-out shapes, put them in the oven for 30 minutes; switch trays on the racks midway through baking.

While they are baking, you can work on rolling and cutting the rest of the dough, if you've decided to use all of the dough today. When you take the cookies out, place the tray on a cooling rack. Keep baked and cooled treats in a sealed container in the fridge if your cookies have meat in them. If not, you can keep them in a jar on your counter.

Luna's Liver-Lovin' Cookies

Lovin' Life with my liver treats!

✳ Ingredients
½ lb chicken livers
2 medium carrots, roughly cut into 1" to 2" pieces
1 cup chopped spinach or kale
1⅓ TBSP flaxseed, ground
3 cups whole wheat flour—I recommend King Arthur's
      (if using gluten-free flour, use approximately 3 ¾ cups)
½ cup rolled oats
1 egg

✳ Supplies
baking sheets
parchment paper or silpat

✳ Instructions
1. Preheat oven to 350 degrees.

2. Place cut carrots in food processor and process until carrots are shredded. Add chicken livers and egg to shredded carrots in food processor until well combined.

3. Using an electric mixer, combine flour, oats and flaxseed, and blend on low for 20 seconds. Then, add cut greens and food-processed liver mixture to dry mixture in electric mixer, and blend on low until it forms a ball.

4. Sprinkle handful of flour on clean counter or large cutting board. Add mixture and sprinkle more flour on top. Using rolling pin, roll out until ¼" thick or slightly less. Make sure that while rolling out the dough, you flip it at least once, so it doesn't stick to surface; if the dough starts sticking to the rolling pin, add more flour.

Luna's Liver-Lovin' Cookies continued

5. Using cookie cutter or a small drinking glass, cut out pieces of the rolled-out dough and place pieces on baking sheet lined with parchment paper or silpat.

6. Place filled cookie sheets in preheated oven and bake for 20 minutes.

7. Let baked pieces cool on cooling rack before giving to your pooch. Keep refrigerated because of the chicken livers.

Variation on the Typical Kong Filler

If you put peanut butter in KONG dog toys, here's a healthier and tastier version that even *you* can eat. Using a steamer, steam five large carrots for an hour until they're very soft. Let them cool.

Then, mash the carrots with one cup of organic peanut butter, ¼ cup honey and one teaspoon of cinnamon. Mix well and add some of this mixture to your dog's Kong.

It's delicious! My dog Shelby didn't like peanut butter OR carrots, but she loved this mixture!

Sardine Puffs

Two paws up on this recipe for a fantastic snack!

✳ Ingredients

2 cups whole wheat flour
  (or, use 2½ cups of gluten-free flour)
1 egg
½ tsp. baking soda
one 4 to 4.5 oz can of boneless sardines packed in water
½ cup applesauce
½ cup water
2 TBSP gelatinous chia seeds (see p. 16)

✳ Supplies

mixer or food processor
two to three baking sheets

✳ Instructions

1. Preheat oven to 350 degrees.

2. Add all of the ingredients to a standing mixer, including the water from the can of sardines.

3. Mix on medium for two minutes. While mixer is running, line the baking sheets with parchment paper or a silpat. The mixture needs to be thick enough to hold its shape; add more flour if too runny.

4. Depending on the size of your dog, use a teaspoon or tablespoon to scoop the mixture onto the baking sheet. If you're feeling fancy, you could use a pastry bag! The mixture doesn't spread, so place spoonfuls of mixture within a ½ inch to one inch of each other.

5. Bake for 30 minutes, switching the pans between racks after the first 15 minutes of baking. Cool before you share with your pup. Refrigerate leftovers.

Barkin' Baklava
Your dogs will be barkin' for more!

✳ **Ingredients**
2 cups almond flour
½ cup honey, divided in half
2 TBSP flaxseed, ground
1 cup blueberries
1 egg
¼ cup of water or coconut water

✳ **Supplies**
9x9-inch baking pan
food processor or blender (or will need to vigorously stir)

✳ **Instructions**
1. Preheat oven to 350 degrees.

2. Add ¼ cup of honey (leaving other ¼ cup for later) and all other ingredients to food processor. Process for 30 seconds to a minute, until mixture is a thicker texture similar to cooked oatmeal.

3. Lightly oil 9x9-inch baking pan, and dust with flour. Pour mixture in pan and spread evenly.

4. Drizzle remaining ¼ cup of honey over top of mixture in pan.

5. Bake for 30 minutes. Cut into smaller, treat-size pieces. Always cool before serving.

Healthy Belly Cookies

*Make your dog's belly **and** taste buds happy!*

✳ Ingredients

one 15-ounce can 100% pure pumpkin
2 eggs
one 15-ounce can garbanzo beans, rinsed and drained
½ tsp. baking soda
4 cups spinach torn into pieces, then wilted
1 TBSP olive oil
2 TBSP gelatinous chia seeds (see p. 16)
2 cups whole wheat flour (if using gluten-free flour, 2½ cups)
one 14.5 oz can salmon *or* one pound cooked hamburger
    or ground turkey, drained

✳ Supplies

two to three baking sheets
large skillet and stirring utensil
parchment paper or silpat

✳ Instructions

1. Preheat oven to 350 degrees. Cover two baking sheets with silpat or parchment paper.

2. Add oil to a large skillet and heat on medium. Once skillet is hot, add spinach and cook until wilted and move to bowl. If using hamburger or turkey, brown in the same skillet, and drain and dispose of grease.

3. In a food processor, add pumpkin and garbanzo beans. Process for one minute until thoroughly combined. Then, add flour, eggs and baking soda; mix for additional minute to thoroughly combine. Add salmon or hamburger, chia seeds and cooked spinach and use short bursts with the food processor to mix ingredients but **not** fully purée.

4. Using a teaspoon or tablespoon, depending if you want smaller or larger treats, **or** using a pastry bag, place mounds of the mixture an inch apart on baking sheets. This mixture will not spread.

Healthy Belly Cookies continued

5. Bake at 350 degrees for 20-30 minutes, switching pans halfway through if on upper and lower racks. Cool and feed immediately to hungry hounds.

It's Not Just
About the Walk

Some days are better than others, even for our dogs. If you have one of those days, due to your schedule, inclement weather or low energy, and you just can't get your pups out for that last walk, try some of these ideas for keeping your dogs active and happy, mentally and physically.

If your dog loves the car, take him/her out for a short ride. If your dog likes other dogs, set up a play date! The level of exercise and excitement your dog gets from playing with other dogs is hard to match. There are also some great interactive toys that entertain and require your dog to roll the toy in order for small treats to fall out and reward your dog. Additionally, you can create a game with a muffin pan: Put small-size treats in *some* or all of the muffin cups and place a tennis ball in each cup, so your dog has to search for the treats. They will love these fun, stimulating experiences!

Natural Nutty Cookies

*Ready to make a fast, healthy treat for your own pooch —
or as a gift for a furry friend?*

✳ Ingredients

½ cup organic creamy peanut butter
½ cup unsweetened applesauce
2 tsp. cinnamon
1 egg
1 ripe banana
1 cup water
2 cups whole wheat flour (if using gluten-free flour, 2½ cups)
4 TBSP gelatinous chia seeds (see p. 16)

✳ Supplies

large mixing bowl and mixing utensil
cookie sheets
rolling pin
parchment paper or silpat

✳ Instructions

1. Preheat oven to 350 degrees.

2. Put all ingredients in food processor; process for about one to two minutes until smooth. Mixture will be slightly sticky and tacky to the touch. Line baking sheet with parchment paper or silpat.

3. Spread mixture on baking sheet in a thin layer to the edges of the sheet. Bake for one hour. After baking, mixture will be slightly harder and browner around edges and softer towards the middle.

4. Cool and break into pieces. Store in an airtight container or bag, only after cookies have *completely* cooled; if you want these treats to last longer, refrigerate. I use the crispy, outside part for training treats and the softer middle pieces for at-home treats.

"Ever consider what they must think of us? I mean,
here we come back from the grocery store with the
most amazing haul--chicken, pork, half a cow.
They must think we are the greatest hunters on earth!"
Anne Tyler

  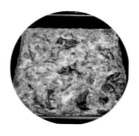

Recipes

Main Meals
and Kibble Mix-Ins

Comfortable Meet-and-Greet

In Dogville, staring dogs in the eyes and hovering over them may make some dogs feel uncomfortable. Some dogs, especially small dogs, can feel overwhelmed and trapped if you bend over the top of their head to pet them. Signs that dogs are stressed in these situations can include the following behaviors: licking their lips, shaking their fur, tucking their tail between their legs, and pulling their head back into their shoulders. When approaching new dogs, offer an open hand, palm up, towards their nose, so they can sniff you and determine if they want further interaction. Don't force it--trust the dog's signals.

Tell kids that it is always up to the dog if he/she wants to be friends. Some good approaches with new dogs include the following: avert your eyes, turn your head away from the dog, and hold out your hand, so the dog can approach in a manner that feels comfortable. Avoid leaning over the dog, as this can feel threatening, and do not pull on a dog's ears or tail or startle the dog. If the dog doesn't seem interested in being friends, discontinue trying to engage the dog. Allow the dog to engage on his/her terms. **PLEASE: Never allow a child to put his/her face in front of a strange dog's face.**

Tilly's Cauliflower, Sweet Potato and Turkey Mash

This recipe makes a great topping for your sweetie's kibble!
It's also good if you are trying to get some weight off of your pooches —
this recipe will fill them up without high-calorie or fat content.

✳ Ingredients
1 head cauliflower
1 large yam or orange sweet potato
1½ lbs lean ground turkey
2 tsp. fennel seeds

✳ Supplies
vegetable steamer
potato masher or fork

✳ Instructions
1. Steam the cauliflower and sweet potato for one hour until soft enough to mash.

2. While the veggies are steaming, brown the ground turkey. Let cool.

3. Mash the steamed and softened cauliflower and sweet potato with a potato masher or fork. Let cool.

4. Combine cooled mashed vegetables, cooled ground turkey and fennel seeds, and mix well. *For an additional nutritional punch,* you may add two tablespoons of gelatinous chia seeds (see p. 16) or ground flaxseed (see p. 11).

Forrest's Favorite Frittata

This is an egg-cellent recipe with plenty of protein!

✻ Ingredients
3 eggs
3 cups egg whites (I use a carton of 100% liquid egg whites,
usually organic)
½ pound chicken livers
1 cup *cooked* quinoa (optional)
1 cup steamed or raw broccoli, cut into small pieces
3 TBSP gelatinous chia seeds (see p. 16)

✻ Supplies
9x9-inch baking pan, sprayed with canola or olive oil
mixing bowl and whisk

✻ Instructions
1. Preheat oven to 350 degrees.

2. Cook the chicken livers. Let cool.

3. Combine eggs, egg whites, broccoli, chia seeds and cooked quinoa—only
if you're adding quinoa—in bowl. Whisk to combine well.

4. Cut cooled liver in small pieces and add to egg mixture. Mix well.

5. Spray a 9x9-inch pan with canola or olive oil. Pour mixture into
pan. Bake for 35 minutes.

6. Cool. Cut into squares.

Healthy Heart Meal

No cooking required!
All ingredients support the heart.

✳ Ingredients
2 TBSP almonds, crushed
1 can tuna (5 oz.) or salmon (4-5 oz.), in water
1 apple, thinly sliced
1 TBSP extra virgin olive oil

✳ Supplies
mixing bowl and spoon or fork

✳ Instructions
Combine all ingredients and add your preferred amount to kibble.

That's it!

Harley's Happy Tummy Bake

Does your pooch typically or temporarily have a sensitive tummy?
These ingredients are extra-easy on the stomach.

✳ **Ingredients**

1 large yam or sweet potato
½ cup blueberries
1 tsp. fresh, grated ginger
2 TBSP plain yogurt
2 TBSP gelatinous chia seeds (see p. 16)
one 15-ounce can 100% pure pumpkin
½ cup rolled oats
20 ounces extra lean ground turkey, beef or bison

✳ **Supplies**

9x9x2-inch baking pan
fork or potato masher
mixing bowls

✳ **Instructions**

1. Preheat oven to 350 degrees.

2. With a fork, poke yam/sweet potato in several areas—no exploding potatoes, please! Either cook in microwave on high at six minutes or bake in oven at 425 degrees for an hour to 75 minutes (whenever potato is super-soft when poked with fork, all the way to the middle). Let cool.

3. In a large bowl, mix blueberries, ginger, yogurt, pumpkin, raw and lean ground turkey, and oats with your hands or favorite mixing utensil.

4. Once the yam/potato is baked and cool, cut into pieces and mash until soft, using a fork or potato masher. Add to mixture in bowl, along with gelatinous chia seeds. Mix well.

5. Spray a 9x9x2-inch pan with canola or olive oil spray. Spoon and spread mixture into the pan, smoothing the top.

6. Bake for 40 minutes. Cool moderately before serving.

Pumpkin Turkey Pie

No baking involved!

✳ Ingredients
1 TBSP olive oil
20 oz lean ground turkey
2 cups fresh greens, shredded, such as kale, spinach, swiss chard
one 15-ounce can 100% pure pumpkin

Optional: ½ cup quinoa or oats, cooked

✳ Supplies
large skillet and mixing spoon
small stove pot to cook quinoa

✳ Instructions
1. If adding *optional* quinoa, start cooking according to directions, so it is ready when other steps are completed.

2. Add olive oil to large skillet and set to medium heat. Always allow skillet to warm oil for two to three minutes before adding the meat, for proper browning and even cooking.

3. Add turkey to the heated and oiled skillet. Cook turkey thoroughly and add two cups of greens. Stir until greens are wilted.

4. Add one can of pumpkin and stir well. Then, if you're adding quinoa or oats, this is the time to do it. Stir well.

5. Turn off burner and remove pan from heat. Let cool. This mixture will be somewhat soft, so mix into or spoon onto your dog's kibble.

Salmon Loaf

Quick + Simple + Salmon = Happy You, Happy Dog

✳ Ingredients
Two 14.75-oz. cans salmon, drained
One 14-oz. can no-sodium garbanzo beans, drained
1 stalk of fresh broccoli
2 tsp. fennel seeds, whole
1 tsp. grated ginger
1 apple, sliced thinly
2 eggs

✳ Supplies
large mixing bowl and mixing utensil
meatloaf pan, such as or similar to 9½" X 5½" X 2½"

✳ Instructions
1. Preheat oven to 350 degrees.

2. Cut stalk of fresh broccoli into small pieces, until you have about a cup of chopped broccoli. You may not need the whole stem.

3. Drain can of garbanzo beans and purée in food processor for 30 seconds until smooth. Add puréed beans, cut broccoli and drained cans of salmon to bowl.

4. Add fennel seeds and choice of other seed to the mixing bowl. Lastly, add one egg to the bowl to bind.

5. Mix all ingredients with your hands, spoon or spatula. Then, spoon mixture into lightly greased meatloaf pan.

6. Bake for 40 minutes and cool before feeding your hungry hounds!

Refrigerate leftovers in a sealed storage container.

Mini's Mama Mia Meatballs

*Mini says, "I like meat, and I love chasing balls....
what could be better than meatballs?"*

✳ Ingredients

2-2½ lbs of ground meat, i.e. turkey,
   bison, hamburger or a combination
2 eggs
1⅓ TBSP flaxseed, ground
⅓ cup of blueberries
½ cup cooked quinoa, if gluten free, or oats

Optional: handful of raw greens, such as kale or spinach, diced

✳ Supplies

9x13-inch baking pan

✳ Instructions

1. Preheat oven to 350 degrees. Spray 9x13-inch pan with canola oil.

2. Place all ingredients in a medium bowl and mix with your hands.

3. Take approximately 2½ TBSP of the mixture and form into a ball,
   placing balled mixture on baking pan. Repeat for the rest of the mixture,
   placing the balls on the baking sheet with two inches between meatballs.

4. Bake for 40 minutes.

Makes 16-20 meatballs.

Luscious Salmon Muffins

Great for a road trip or picnic with your dog!

✳ Ingredients

3½ cups unbleached whole wheat flour (if using gluten-free flour, add additional ½ cup)

one 14½-ounce canned salmon

1⅓ TBSP flaxseed, ground

1½ cups of kale or spinach, torn into small pieces

1 small or ½ large sweet potato, grated

1 apple, grated

2 eggs

⅓ cup olive oil

½ tsp. turmeric

✳ Supplies

muffin tins—for 12-15 standard-size muffins

cupcake tin liners

✳ Instructions

1. Preheat oven to 350 degrees.

2. Put cupcake papers in a 12-muffin tin or spray muffin tin with canola spray.

3. In a large mixing bowl or electric mixer, mix all ingredients until well blended. Then, fill each muffin tin ⅔ to ¾ full of the blended mixture.

4. Bake muffins for 35 minutes. Cool before serving.

Makes 12-15 muffins.

Refrigerate leftovers in sealed storage containers.

Paw-Lickin' Lasagna

Mama Mia, make me some more!

✳ Ingredients

4 cups of combination of the following—at least two or more of these:
   thinly sliced sweet potatoes, apples, squash and/or zucchini
1½ lbs cooked lean grass fed beef, lamb or bison
one 15-ounce can 100% pure pumpkin
one 15-ounce can garbanzo beans, drained and rinsed
½ cup water
2 TBSP olive oil

✳ Supplies

sharp knife or mandolin
medium-size skillet
9x9-inch baking pan
food processor or blender

✳ Instructions

1. Preheat oven to 350 degrees.

2. Brown meat, drain oil, and set aside pan to cool meat.

3. Thinly slice a mixture of sweet potatoes, apples and squash for a total of four cups. I use a mandolin slicer, but you may also use a knife.

4. Drain and rinse garbanzo beans. In a food processor, add the can of pumpkin and garbanzo beans and ½ cup water. Pureé mixture.

5. Lightly oil a 9x9-inch pan. Layer ⅓ of the sliced veggies/fruits on the bottom, cover with a layer of ⅓ of the pumpkin/bean mixture, and top with ⅓ of the meat. Repeat this layering sequence of ingredients two more times.

6. Bake for 30 minutes. Cool before serving.

Shelby's Sweet and Savory Stew

Get out your crockpot! This makes a lot, so you may want to freeze leftovers.

✳ **Ingredients**
2 TBSP olive oil
2 cups chicken broth
1½ lbs chicken breast and 1½ lbs beef cut in 1-inch pieces
1 large yam or sweet potato
2 carrots
2 apples
1 bunch broccoli

✳ **Supplies**
crockpot
large skillet and stirring utensil

✳ **Instructions**
Total cook time in crockpot: three hours.

1. In a skillet, heat olive oil on medium; allow pan to heat up before adding the three pounds of meat. Brown meat lightly—it seals in the juices. ☺

2. Pour two cups of chicken broth into crockpot and set crockpot on low. Add chopped veggies, sweet potato/yam, apples and browned meat to the crockpot. Cook these ingredients in the crockpot for three hours.

3. Let meal cool before feeding to your best friend.

Refrigerate leftovers.

Skye Boy's Crack Turkey Loaf

When Skye wasn't feeling well, and his appetite was off,
he would always eat his favorite turkey loaf.

✳ Ingredients

2 to 2½ lbs ground turkey—or part turkey, part bison or beef
½ cups rolled oats (optional)
1⅓ TBSP flaxseed, ground
2 TBSP pumpkin seeds, coarsely ground
2 eggs
1 cup your choice of veggies, such as spinach, kale, carrots, squash
1 cup blueberries
1 thinly sliced apple

✳ Supplies

standard loaf pan
large mixing bowl and stirring utensil

✳ Instructions

1. Preheat oven to 350 degrees.

2. Combine all ingredients in large mixing bowl and mix well.

3. Put mixture into loaf pan.

4. Bake one hour.

5. Let loaf cool. When ready to serve, cut into slices.

Refrigerate leftovers.

Jody's Dog Mash

This one is from a friend! Thank you, Jody Christiansen! ☺

✳ Ingredients
4 to 6 skinless, boneless chicken thighs
2 sweet potatoes, steamed or roasted and peeled
½ to 1 cup peas or any preferred vegetable, cooked
1 TBSP olive oil

✳ Supplies
large saucepan with lid
large mixing bowl with stirring utensil
cutting board and knife

✳ Instructions
1. Preheat oven to 350 degrees.

2. After cutting the sweet potatoes into smaller pieces, bake at 350 degrees or steam for approximately 20-30 minutes. Cook the peas or other preferred vegetable according to directions on package.

3. While the sweet potatoes and vegetables (ex. peas) are cooking, cook chicken on stovetop in covered saucepan on medium heat; turn chicken pieces to cook both sides. Once chicken is browned, remove from pan and let rest for several minutes; then, cut into small pieces. Save the chicken juices in the pan to add at the end.

4. Mix the chicken, sweet potatoes, peas and the chicken juice from the pan in a large bowl.

5. Serve to your best friend—YUM!

Store the remaining mix in a sealed container in the refrigerator.

Recipes

Special Occasion

"He is your friend, your partner, your defender, your dog.
You are his life, his love, his leader. He will be yours,
faithful and true, to the last beat of his heart.
You owe it to him to be worthy of such devotion."
Author Unknown

Holiday Stew

While you and your family are enjoying your holiday meal, make this delicious recipe for your canine, so there's no begging at your holiday table!

✳ Ingredients
2-2 ½ lbs chicken or turkey thighs and drumsticks
1 cup frozen or fresh cranberries
1 large sweet potato or russet potato, diced
1½ cup fresh string beans
1 cup chicken broth, no salt

Optional: 1 TBSP fennel seeds

✳ Supplies
crock-pot
large skillet
large, slotted spoon

✳ Instructions
1. Brown the chicken or turkey parts; then, add to crock-pot with the rest of ingredients. Cook on low for four hours.

2. Using a slotted, large spoon, take chicken out of crock-pot and **remove bones and skin** from chicken. Bones must be removed, in order to avoid a choking hazard for your dog; removing the skin is highly advised, as it's very fatty. Add skinless and boneless chicken back to crock-pot and stir with other ingredients.

3. Cool to room temperature before feeding to your pooch.

Shelby and Skye's Birthday Wedding Cake Recipe

This recipe also includes the frosting! Add candles and sing, bark or bay!

✳ **Ingredients: Cake**
  2 cups whole wheat flour
    (if using gluten-free flour, 2 ½ cups)
  1 tsp. baking soda
  2 tsp. ground cinnamon
  ½ cup applesauce
  1 large egg, beaten
  2 TBSP pumpkin seeds
    or chia seeds, ground
  1 cup 100% pure pumpkin
  1 cup hot water

✳ **Ingredients: Frosting**
  2 sweet potatoes
  2 carrots
  1 lb of lean ground
    turkey, chicken,
    beef or lamb
  1 tsp. turmeric
  ½ cup plain yogurt

✳ **Supplies**
  9x13-inch glass or metal baking pan
  three medium to large mixing bowls
  large skillet and stirring utensil
  electric mixer (optional)
  birthday candles (optional)

✳ **Instructions: Cake**
1. Preheat oven to 350 degrees.

> **Save time:** Steam the sweet potatoes and carrots
> for the frosting, while you're making the cake.

2. Grease the bottom and sides of a 13x9-inch glass or metal pan.

3. Combine flour, baking soda and cinnamon in medium bowl.

4. In electric mixer or separate large bowl, add oats, applesauce, egg and seeds (ground pumpkin or chia seeds). Mix for one minute on medium speed in electric mixer or several minutes if mixing by hand. Add the flour, baking soda and cinnamon mixture; mix until thoroughly combined.

Shelby and Skye's Birthday Wedding Cake Recipe continued
Instructions: Cake

5. Add pumpkin and hot water to main mixture. Mix until thoroughly combined.

6. Pour into greased 9x13 inch pan and bake for 45 minutes. Cool on a rack before frosting.

✳ Instructions: Frosting

1. Steam two sweet potatoes and two carrots for an hour. Then, let cool.

2. Brown one pound of lean ground turkey, chicken, beef or lamb in skillet. Cool.

3. In a large bowl, mash cooled, steamed veggies with a fork or potato masher. Add cooled, browned ground meat, turmeric and yogurt. Mix well.

4. Spread frosting on cooled cake.

5. Add candles and wag, sing, bark or bay.

Refrigerate any uneaten portions and use within several days.

What will you create?

Once you've created some of these recipes and have greater knowledge of ideal textures and how ingredients work together, you can start creating your own recipes.

A good place to start, if you're feeling a little uncertain, is taking one of my recipes and replacing certain ingredients that you would like to use—and seeing what happens…. and especially what makes your hound happy. ☺

If You're on the Run and
Don't Have Time to Cook...

Don't have time to make a full recipe or want to more quickly add some extra nutritional value to your pooch's kibble? See the following tips for some ideas. Adding the prepared vegetables, as detailed below, is a fast, easy way to boost your dog's kibble and guarantee a happy dog at mealtime.

Plan Ahead for Upcoming Menu

- **Chia Seeds**: Soak one part chia seeds to four parts water and store gelatinous chia seeds (see p. 16) in refrigerator. Then, when you need them for your recipe, they are ready to go.

- **Vegetables**
  Roast: It's great to throw some veggies in the oven to roast, so you have them on hand, such as broccoli, cauliflower, brussel sprouts, kale, carrots, apples, butternut or spaghetti squash. Preheat oven to 400 degrees. Put upper rack towards top of oven. Lightly coat a baking pan with coconut or olive oil, spread with veggies and place in preheated oven. Roast for 20-30 minutes. Then, put these roasted veggies in a storage container, so you can add them to any meal you create during the week.

  Bake: Instead of roasting, you can also bake your veggies ahead of time. Just preheat your oven to 350 degrees and bake on a middle or lower rack for 30-40 minutes.

  Steam: Steaming your veggies is faster yet. Steam the veggies you need for about 20 minutes, or until you're able to poke a fork through the vegetable easily. Use right away or store in fridge.

Quicker Substitutes

▪ Use "ready" (canned), quick, healthy proteins like sardines, anchovies and salmon. Or, use an organic rotisserie chicken and remove the skin, instead of cooking raw chicken yourself.

   Roasted or baked veggies can be added to high-quality kibble, oats or rice; add a healthy protein, and you'll have a happy dog at mealtime.

• Spaghetti squash is an excellent, nutritional, low-starch vegetable. Cut it lengthwise in half, brush olive oil inside cut halves, and place on baking sheet face down. Roast or bake for 45 minutes at 400 degrees. After roasting/baking, you can shred the squash with a fork, which has a pasta-like consistency to it. Makes a great mix-in for your dog's kibble! **Bonus Tip:** This makes a lot! Share some of this squash with your diggity-dog and use the squash for your own meal as a pasta replacement. Add marinara and veggies or meatballs... *voilà*!

Pet Insurance Recommended

At some point your beloved dog will probably get injured or ill, and it can cost thousands of dollars. I highly recommend getting pet insurance as soon as you get your dog. You can price-shop different companies, but I have had a very good experience with VPI Pet Insurance, now known as Nationwide®. I usually get the most comprehensive insurance plan, plus a cancer rider. Rarely do our dogs die of old age, in their sleep. With every dog I've had, I've been grateful that I've invested in pet insurance.

The Love Story of Shelby and Skye: Part Two

"We are together now. That's all that matters.
And when the time comes, you will still be with me.
And I will be with you."

Author Unknown

Let Them Eat Cake!
Skye and Shelby's Birthday Wedding

When my friend Missy was visiting in the summer of 2013 with her boys Max and Will, they fell in love with Shelby and Skye. Skye had been been diagnosed with an illness earlier that year, and we were hoping he would make it to his birthday in September, when he would be 12 years old.

Max and Will, ages eight and nine at the time, made me promise them that since Shelby and Skye loved each other, they would get married. So, Diana—Skye's mom—and I decided if Skye made it to his birthday, we would marry the dogs.

The happy day came, and not only was Skye alive and kicking, but he also was thriving. We had a get-together and dressed Shelby in a veil and Skye in a bow tie, and they promptly became "man and wife" amid much hilarity. I had gotten ordained as a minister earlier in 2013 to marry two friends of mine that summer, so the wedding was performed by a licensed minister—me.

"I don't want you to see me before the ceremony," said Shelby.

Party time!

After the wedding, we had the reception/birthday party with food, cake and lots of presents for Skye. The pictures show how happy they were!

Shelby and Skye: Love Eternal

In February 2013, Diana received the devastating news that Skye had hemangiosarcoma, a tumor in his heart. Diana and Rick were heartbroken, but determined to make his time left the best ever. A year later, his vets could not believe how well he was doing, as they had initially given him a couple months to live at best. During his last couple of months, Shelby was by his side no matter what. She was even with him when he passed on March 30, 2014.

Cheryl and Shelby

Thirteen days later, when Shelby wasn't eating as usual and didn't seem to be herself, I took her to the vet for a check-up. They found a tumor in her spleen and removed it on April 12. We were elated when we were told later that week that they hadn't found cancer in her tumor. We rejoiced and felt relieved that we had several more good years ahead of us.

Alas, on May 7, Shelby woke up, had her usual cuddling with me and my husband, but then she shrieked in pain. We took her to the ER, and they said there was nothing they could do. Her liver had bled because she *indeed* had cancer in her spleen—contrary to what we were initially told, and it had moved to her liver. We cried and sat with her and told her how much we loved her.

Skye, Ken and Shelby

Shelby and Laurie

Aunties Laurie and Diana came and said goodbye, then we said a final goodbye to our precious girl. Five weeks after her beloved SkyeBoy passed, she just couldn't stand life without him, and she joined him in heaven. While the vet may have said Shelby died of cancer, I say she died of a broken heart. We miss these amazing dogs and feel such gratitude and admiration for their love and all they taught us. **Shelby's and Skye's love continues… in our hearts infinitely.**

Rest in Peace, Our Beautiful Angels

"Goodbyes are only for those who love with their eyes.
Because for those who love with heart and soul,
there is no such thing as separation."

Rumi

Organizations That Make
a Doggone Difference

"I shall pass through this world but once.
Any good therefore that I can do or
any kindness that I can show to
any fellow creature,
let me do it now.
Let me not defer or neglect it,
for I shall not pass this way again."

Stephen Grellet

The Magic of PC's Pantry
Boulder, Colorado USA

Colleen and Mary Lee

Owning a store has never been a dream of mine, but every time I walk into PC's Pantry, I think, "If I ever owned a store, I would want one just like this." Mary Lee Withers is the owner, and her right-hand woman is Colleen Smith. Together they run the show. The store is 5000 square feet and has every food and supply imaginable for dogs and cats, and Mary Lee brings most of her dogs and cats to work every day.

Customers are allowed to bring their dogs into the store, and at any given time, there are excited diggity dogs, vying for a cookie from Mary Lee and Colleen. It is BIG FUN for you and your dog to have an outing to PC's Pantry!

Shelby would nudge the other dogs out of the way, so Colleen could throw bits of cookies in the air that Shelby would snap up every time. Shelby and Colleen were quite a team with this trick.

Since PC's Pantry opened in 1998, Mary Lee has given me and countless others invaluable advice. I swear she is one small step down from being an actual vet! She has helped me figure out so many perplexing issues with my dogs over the years.

You would be hard-pressed to find another person that cares about animals as much as Mary Lee. The food and treats she sells are top quality and healthy. If you're buying kibble or canned food, she is the person who will direct you to exactly what you need. Even though I make my own dog food, I add it to the excellent kibble I get from PC's. Mary Lee has helped numerous people with the care and surgery of their ailing animals. Her compassion for the suffering of animals is bottomless. I am a fan!

Learn more about PC's Pantry on-line: http://pcspantry.com.

The Humane Society

I started volunteering at the Humane Society of Boulder Valley in January 2007. I started as a dog kennel assistant, which includes walking the dogs in the adoption center. After several years, I was asked to participate in the GADAB (Give a Dog a Bone) program, which requires walking the dogs that are not ready for the adoption floor yet, such as dogs that are receiving behavioral support, sick or injured dogs, and fearful dogs.

I have had many people over the years ask me, "How can you do that? I would be so sad being around all of these homeless dogs. I just don't think I could do it!" It makes me think about my beloved Shelby; within two weeks of starting my volunteering at the Humane Society, I had adopted Shelby. She was found in Pagosa Springs as a stray, was in a shelter there for two to three weeks, and was then transferred to the Humane Society of Boulder Valley, where she resided for an additional week until we adopted her.

I feel such gratitude to the wonderful people who volunteer, whether walking the dogs, doing the laundry, filling KONGs with peanut butter... there are so many things lovely volunteers do! All of those tasks combined kept Shelby safe, fed, walked and loved, and she had a warm blanket to sleep on, a tennis ball and toy to play with, and food in her belly, until she could find her forever home.

I have often thought that if you are considering doing volunteer work, volunteer for what tugs on your heart. I think whatever cause that may be for you is where you can best spend your energy and/or dollars.

One of the added bonuses of volunteering is meeting amazing people. It's such a community! I have to give a shout-out to my GADAB partner, Carol Haraway. I love this woman! We have worked together for many years on Thursday mornings, starting with the adoption center then moving over to GADAB. She and I are like a tactical team together, deciding what needs to be done, and getting all of the dogs taken care of efficiently and lovingly. Carol is funny, smart and caring, and she tells it like it is. She has also helped with training classes, kennel transfers, vet clinic and dog video filming. I can always count on her; Carol is rock solid.

Another great woman I have become friends with is Andy Merryman. She is a diehard volunteer, doing everything from making videos of the dogs, traveling to other shelters to transfer dogs to Boulder, and training harder-to-handle dogs. Now a certified dog trainer, she is so kind and such an animal lover! I am grateful to call this woman a friend.

I am so proud to be associated with the Humane Society of Boulder Valley. The knowledge I have gained volunteering here has been invaluable. What I have gained far exceeds what I have given. Employees and volunteers are all top-notch and extremely caring, and I think the Humane Society of Boulder Valley is one of the best-run shelters in the United States.

Learn more about the Humane Society of Boulder Valley at http://boulderhumane.org.

The Next Generation

"Dogs come into our lives to teach us about love;
they depart to teach us about loss.
A new dog never replaces an old dog;
it merely expands the heart.
If you have loved many dogs, your heart is very big."
E. Jong

Dixie, Mabel and Romie

About the Author

As a massage therapist for 20 years, Cheryl Bauer has also integrated acutonics, crystology and reiki into her sessions. She lived in the DC area for most of her life and then moved to Boulder, where she lives with her husband Ken and their dogs. Cheryl and her husband love to cook and have taken cooking classes through Escoffier School of Culinary Arts.

As a young girl, Cheryl and her brother collected dogs and cats from their neighborhood and brought them into their home on weekend mornings to play with and enjoy. When she was six, Cheryl was gifted an Easy-Bake Oven, and, well, now as an adult, she's combining two of her long-time favorites—dogs and baking/cooking—and teaches classes and develops resources for feeding healthy food to dogs and loving these pets unconditionally.

Learn more about Cheryl and her Cookin' for Your Canine classes, products and other goodies at http://10DogsLater.com.

Cheryl Teaches Classes!

Have fun and experience hands-on
cooking classes, so you can be inspired
and guided as you cook for your diggity dogs!

Learn more at
www.10DogsLater.com

Index